On the Water Meridian

*For Ginny —
longtime friend
of Rosie's —*

Barbara

On the Water Meridian

poems by
Barbara Bloom

Hummingbird Press
Santa Cruz, California

Copyright © 2007 by Barbara Bloom

All rights reserved. No part of this book may be reproduced in any manner without permission in writing, except for brief quotations in reviews and articles.

Library of Congress Control Number: 2007926034
ISBN#13: 978-0-9792567-1-4   ISBN #10: 0-9792567-1-2

Acknowledgement is made to the following publications for poems originally appearing in them, sometimes in an earlier version:
A Cadence of Hooves: A Celebration of Horses: "Omeline"
American Land Forum: "Cormorants"
Bellowing Ark: "Sixth Grade Science," "Divorce," "Sleeping with You"
Green Fuse: "Through the Fire"
Lighthouse Point: An Anthology of Santa Cruz Writers: "Luther Burbank Gardens"
Porter Gulch Review: "Home," "Mars"
Quarry West: "The Horse Trainer's Advice"
Southern Poetry Review: "Nineteen"
Sou'wester: "Cod-Jigging," "Lake Wilderness"
Sow's Ear: "September 12, 2001"

The author thanks for their steadfast encouragement, both in the life and in the work: Gilbert and Kathryn Bloom, who set me on this path; my daughter, Kathryn Gailson; Carl Bloom and Diane Zipperman; Elizabeth Ramstead and John Dark; Morton Marcus, my first poetry teacher; William Stafford; Mary Lonnberg Smith; Naomi Clark; Joseph Stroud and the members of his ongoing workshop; the Hummingbird poets, Len Anderson, Charles Atkinson, Ken Weisner, David Sullivan, Debra Spencer, Rosie King, Tilly Shaw, George Lober, Joanna Martin, Amber Sumrall, and Maggie Paul; John and Wilma Chandler; Joan Safajek; Ana Chou; Margie Robatto; Kathleen Roberts; all my students, past and present, who have taught me over and over again the importance of writing what is real and true; Paula Jones and Ellery Akers, my dearest friends; and especially my husband, Fred Winterbottom, without whose love and support none of this could have happened.

Cover and frontispiece photos by Gilbert Bloom
Author photo by Mati Messager
Graphic design by Kathleen Roberts
InDesign by Ken Weisner and David Sullivan

HUMMINGBIRD PRESS
2299 Mattison Lane
Santa Cruz, CA
95062-1821

Printed by Bookmobile

for Fred and Kathryn

CONTENTS

I. Holding Fast

On the High Sierra Loop, 1960	11
Not Science	12
Untamed Lands	13
Magnetic Force	14
Luther Burbank Gardens	15
Star Cards	16
Multiplication: The Sevens	17
Sixth Grade Science	18
Omeline	19
Through the Fire	20
The Horse Trainer's Advice	21
My Canada	22
Cod-Jigging	24
At the Bow Watch	26
The Unlived Life	27
True North	28

II. Mountains That Cannot Be Worn Away

Powell River News	33
That Letter	35
Switchboard Operator, Ahwahnee Hotel	36
Nineteen	37
The Soldier	39
Professor Miller's Office Hour	41
File Clerk	42
After	43
Divorce	44
Crossing the Mountains with Blitzen	45
Rehearsing Love	46

Her Legacy	48
At the Begonia Gardens	50
The Cottage	52
On the Water Meridian	54
The Singer	55
Chinese Food in Calgary	56
Villa le Rondini	58
Sleeping with You	59
Home	60

III. What the Rain Has Touched

Encounter	65
What I Know About the End of the World	66
When	68
Long Distance from Jerusalem	69
Mars	70
Orion	72
Making Things Right	74
Mother	75
The Message	76
September 12, 2001	78
Looking Up "Ranunculus"	80
At Lake Margaret, Again	81
Lake Wilderness	82
Natural History	83
Cormorants	84
Nine Days	85
With Reptiles	86
Evidence	87
Vancouver to Edmonton	89

I.

Holding Fast

On the High Sierra Loop, 1960

What my mother recorded in the faded journal
are the weights of our backpacks,
how many miles we walked each day,
the number of fish we caught,
and sometimes, weather.

"Rained and hailed—
took refuge in fine cave during first shower.
Had previously been occupied." Yes, I remember
the lightning flashes,
my brother and I counting the seconds, "one-thousand-and-one,
one-thousand-and-two" until the thunder crashed,
my sister Elizabeth crying, and then
huddling together in the cave,
my father pulling a hunk of dark chocolate from his pack,
passing it around, and my mother
taking Elizabeth on her lap
and saying, "Soon you'll be snug as a bug in a rug."

You'd have to know my mother
to know how unlike her this was,
so I never forgot her saying that,
even if it wasn't for me. Of course,
stumbling on this notebook now, I wonder
about the cave—how did my mother know
it had been occupied? And by what?
Bear? Man? Mountain lion?

Of those weeks in the mountains,
I don't remember catching the fish,
or the day-long trudges between High Sierra camps.
But I remember my mother cradling my sister,
and the way the rain stopped suddenly,
everything smelling of pine and dust.

Not Science

I knew I could never like science enough
to please my father,
though my brother and I
would go into his lab with its cool floor
and play with his instruments.
We especially liked the oscilloscope,
how it took our voices
and made them into wavy green lines,
and we practiced saying "ooohh" and "aahhh" and "w."
"W" was the best,
because it made little "w"s on the screen,
and that seemed like magic to us.

We were told
only to believe what could be measured and proven.
God, the Easter Bunny, and Santa Claus
were dismissed in the same sentence
as hooey, just like fairy tales.

I read all the fairy tales,
and prepared my three wishes
just in case I should ever be asked
what three things I most desired.
Riding my horse through the woods
or across sunny fields dotted with spreading tanbark oaks,
I felt something
the instruments in my father's lab
could not have picked up.
I didn't know what it was,
or even that I had strayed outside
the careful world of science,
but I let the reins go slack,
and we steered for it.

Untamed Lands

When my father thought we weren't around,
he'd walk into our rooms
and just stand there
as if trying to remember something important
or think what it was he left behind
in among our dolls and baseball gloves.
I never dared to ask him
what it was he was looking for,
though I think I knew even then—
some little whiff of who we were,
his children.

Of course, he might have tried to talk to us
and found out that way,
but I don't think he trusted us to know,
so instead he stood in our rooms
as if they were countries he longed to visit,
like the untamed lands in our *National Geographics*,
and, like those places,
he would just have to steal a look
from outside.

Magnetic Force

I stood on the cement floor
of the basement lab room,
wrapping wires around a metal bar
while my father looked on,
beaming. He was glad, he said,
to see me finally taking an interest
in science. His calendar, a nude
Marilyn Monroe posed against red velvet,
hung on one wall. She, too, seemed
to be taking an interest, her glance
directed at the open toolbox,
the mirror on the lid, green felt lining—
almost like a jewelry case—
and the carefully arranged tools,
smelling of metal.

When we finished, the rotor spun,
as it was meant to, opposites
rushing towards each other, similar poles
pushing back. Just then, my brother
rode by the open window on his bike,
and I raced out the door,
spinning away from that cold room
and the person my father longed for me to be.

Luther Burbank Gardens

Running my hands over the smooth
leaves of the cactus
I remember my father told me
how Burbank talked to the cacti,
explained to them
that they no longer needed their thorns:
he would protect them now.
Scientists could not understand
how he developed this spineless variety,
and he did not tell them
about those walks at night
through the gardens
whispering to the plants—
and how they listened to him
and willingly shed their spines.

Star Cards

Green stars meant something bad:
you hadn't finished your vegetables
or had left some chore undone. Red
were just okay—nothing special,
nothing bad either. Silver stars,
worth a dime each: above
and beyond. Gold, best of all,
and worth twenty cents.

So we toiled to be good,
to have our star cards
shimmer gold and silver. It was
our father's idea, the star system,
like all our systems. Every night
before bed, our mother would review
our days, then lick a colored star
and paste it on our cards:
seven stars a week.
Sundays, we did not go to church,
but we cashed in our row of stars
for a few dimes.

How I longed for those shiny dimes,
Franklin Roosevelt or the winged Mercury
on the front, the feel of them
in my hand. It was greed
that drove me
to sweep the outside stairs
or iron the big tablecloths.
But even now, I am
haunted by my childish question:
How good was I today?

> *Not quite a gold star.*
> *Not quite enough.*

Multiplication: The Sevens

Those were the ones I never quite learned,
in spite of my third grade teacher, Mrs. Holmes,
pulling me off the playground
on a sunny afternoon when I was deep in a game of two-square,
putting a little spin on the ball
as I served it—and she told me
I'd better learn those times tables
if I ever expected to go on to Grade Four.

I thought most of them were easy, but the sevens
were as wild as my serves,
and though 8 x 8 was always 64,
and 6 x 5 would be 30 every time,
the sevens had their own plan,
and I had to sneak up on them using addition
because you never knew what to expect of 7 x 8
or 7 x 6, and especially 7 x 9,
trickiest of all.

I'd stare at the neat rows of figures
on my plastic pencil box,
trying to force them into my memory,
but some slipped away
like horses intent on avoiding human touch
(because everything always came back to horses
for me then)—
the way they could gallop over hills
to a far pasture, so hidden
even Mrs. Holmes, with her scowling face
and her tapping foot, would never find them.

Sixth Grade Science

I didn't find it strange
that our sixth grade science book
full of experiments and careful explanations
was called *The Boy Scientist*,
and, on the cover, the picture of a boy—
about my age—bending over a beaker,
a look on his face
as if something wonderful
were about to happen.

I'd never wanted to be a girl,
and at eleven I still hoped
I could escape it.
My chest was flat,
my hair short—and I could run as fast
as any boy. The mysteries
of becoming a woman
as presented in the instructional film
the boys were not allowed to see
seemed awful. No,
I planned to stay just how I was.

When the movie ended, we raced
from the darkened room
into the glare of the afternoon playground.
The boys huddled together
at the far end of the baseball diamond,
as if suddenly afraid
to get too close to whatever place it was
we had been
without them.

Omeline

Give me back the smell of Omeline
as I'd open up the burlap sack
and scoop my hands into its sticky sweetness,
my horse stamping impatiently from his stall.

Give me back those afternoons,
stretching out between school and dinner,
when I'd climb up on my horse's back
and we'd go deep into the oak and redwood forests
on the old roads, cantering wherever we could,
and I'd forget where I ended and he started,
and we'd just move through time.

Sometimes I'd take lumps of molasses
from the sweet grainy mix, and suck on them,
before I'd spit them out,
amazed that something that smelled so much like cookies baking
could taste so bitter—then I'd watch my horse
nose deep in his grain, snorting with pleasure,
swishing away a fly or two with his black tail.

How gladly I would walk back down that trail
to the stable, the full bags of grain, my horse,
and being ten years old,
not knowing how much I could ever want this back.

Through the Fire

I dash into the burning barn:
horses scream in fright
and throw themselves against their stalls.
Timbers crack and fall
flaming, around my feet.

I tear off my sweater
and blindfold the horse
farthest from the door,
and though he dances and rears,
I do not falter.
I lead him out to safety,
into the light.

One by one I bring out
every horse.
People grab at me
as I come out, and beg me
not to go back in.
But I don't stop until
I have saved them all.

What I know is that
I am like the horses—
I want a safer way, too,
but there is no other way,
so we come out,
as we must,
through the fire.

The Horse Trainer's Advice

Make your body like a door,
not a wall,
so what he feels
is not that you are something solid
like the fake brick walls
he was beaten to jump—
but that instead,
he can see past you
to the field every horse knows
by smell, by sight,
by the feel of the grass,
and he will approach the door,
curious, unalarmed as you slip the halter on,
his head bent slightly in recognition,
his great heart calm.

My Canada

I traced around the edges of a maple leaf
with red and yellow crayons
and put my carefully written pages together with shiny brads:
Chief Exports, Main Cities, Form of Government, Population,
all copied directly from the encyclopedia at home.
It looked pretty good, I thought—
my first big report, in Mrs. Goodman's class.
I hoped for an A.

So you might have thought I was prepared
when three years later
my father moved us all to Canada.
But my report had not mentioned
how it would feel to leave everything behind,
to say goodbye to my cats and my horse
and live so differently I could hardly find the words
when I wrote letters to my friends in California—
how we took the sailboat across Desolation Sound
to the store and post office
once a week, the only time we saw anyone
outside the family,
living in a place with no roads, no school, no phone,
and almost no money,
just like everyone else up there—
fishing, hunting, growing a big garden,
bald eagles in the treetops,
scream of the gulls over the bay.

The real facts of Canada
came out of the woods and the tides,
cedar tree outside my bedroom window,
steady creak of the oars as we rowed across the bay,
the dark days and long nights of winter, the rain,

the huge summer days—
sinking right through the skin
into some place so deep
it could never be lost.

Cod-Jigging

Past the bluffs of Swimming Point,
we'd ship the oars,
drop in the gleaming, three-pronged lure,
and unwind the fishing line
fathom after fathom.
Then we'd begin to jig
for the deep-dwelling fish.

The little boat would turn and bob,
light on the winter swells,
the hook drifting between jerks,
the snow-covered mountains at the end of the Sound
obscured by clouds.

"Maybe we'll catch a shark,"
my brother would say. "You know,
dogfish *are* shark"—
and whatever we pulled in
came from so far below us,
our arms would be tired with bringing it up
long before we saw it,
but still the fish would fight
when we laid it in the boat,
thrashing between our feet
until my brother knocked it with the gaff.

So little is changed there
except the years
since our childhood.
What we've gained or left behind
seems little more
than the flashing of the lure
in the deep fishing holes,

the ones we believed we were first and only
to find, those secret valleys,
sweetest to the cod,
unmarked on the charts at home.

At the Bow Watch

As the snow fell around the boat
so you couldn't see a thing,
we huddled in the cockpit
thrusting our gloved hands
in the warm stream of diesel exhaust
till they turned black,
and our mother
took the bow watch
to look out for deadheads—
those half-submerged logs
almost invisible below the water,
treacherous to the hull of any boat.

It wasn't until much later
she told us why
she always volunteered for this cold duty:
it was to give herself over to the sensation
of staring straight into those swirling flakes
until the boat was no longer
connected to the earth at all,
but lifted silently off the water.

Then her whole life would fall away
in an instant—her kitchen,
her garden, books, even our voices,
her children, chattering in the stern—
and she floated free.

The Unlived Life

Like a hidden moon
pulling on its planet,
so this other life,
the one I didn't take,
tugs at me. Each day,
driving to work, I pass the barn
with its corrals in front.
I can see the horses bending to their hay
or staring out at the road
in that way they have, heads over the rumps of their friends,
or nose to nose in the companionable silence
of animals. A girl
works a tall bay horse in the arena,
standing on the ground,
lunging the horse in slow, perfect circles.

Shut in the car, I can't smell or hear them,
but I remember my childhood horse,
his deep breaths and the warm smell
of dust and sun and meadows
that rose up when I brushed him.

Then, in a moment, I've passed the barn,
the horses are behind me.
I glance at the dashboard clock:
just enough time to make it to school,
where my students will be filling the room,
pulling out books and notebooks.
When I walk in,
a tall boy in the back corner is bent over his journal,
two girls laugh together and look up,
and just outside, the Japanese maple holds tight
to its impossibly red leaves
in spite of the pull of the wind.

True North

If you are ever lost,
look up in the night sky
for the Big Dipper.
Follow the lip to Polaris:
with the North Star above you,
steer for home.

So my father taught me,
as we leaned out over the porch railing
of the house in British Columbia,
our faces still flushed
from the heat of the fire inside.

I stared at the stars
so close, pulsing.
I couldn't see
how this was ever going to help me.
I wasn't planning to wander off,
especially not here
in this wild place, where bears
and mountain lions
roamed the woods at night.

                              It's true
I've never had to use this advice.
But I know now how easy it is
to lose yourself. My father
has been dead for years, so I can't ask him
if he was offering a simple tip
or if this was supposed to be a metaphor,
the only way
he knew to tell me: *Hold fast*
to what will not shift.
That alone will bring you home.

II.

Mountains That Cannot Be Worn Away

Powell River News
August 5, 1965

We stare out from the yellowed clipping
with its scholarship announcements, our faces serious,
hair carefully arranged. *College-bound,*
the article brags, though a few of the girls
decided to marry instead, and some of the boys
went straight to work at the paper mill.

The local real estate ads
are on the other side:
fixer-uppers and cottages by the sea,
spare bedrooms, full woodshops,
new roofs, deep wells,
must be seen to be believed,
so affordable I am more amazed
at what I might own—
if I could slip back in time—
than what I might say to the girl in the picture,
the one who was me.

I know she had no use
for houses. She was going to travel the world,
be the next Emily Dickinson,
go looking for Heathcliff.

The stiff faces of my graduating class
are keeping their secrets,
and those houses
where we might have awakened
to the sound of a fresh westerly wind
banging the screen door
are long since sold,
and maybe sold again.

But holding this bit of paper in my hands
I wonder if the tide is lapping
at the steps of those cottages now,
or if the Canada geese passing over each fall
still leave a hole in the air
that fills up with our longing.

That Letter

That letter, densely typed
on full-sized paper,
page after page folded together:
a long bike ride along the Fraser River,
your job at the pizza place,
the books you were reading,
the main points carefully summarized,
and then suddenly at the end,
handwritten just before your signature,
words we had never spoken:
I love you.

By the time that letter came,
I was so lost
there in Yosemite—
the overfull waterfalls,
floodwatches on the Merced River,
long nights of a million stars,
and a man who came at me,
saying *marry me, marry me,
you alone can make me whole.*

And my own letter already sent—
I've met someone.
Maybe, somewhere on that thousand miles of coast,
the two planes passed each other,
our lives whirling apart.
Too late to change.
Too late to take things back.

Switchboard Operator, Ahwahnee Hotel

Headset on, I'd plug the cords into the lighted holes.
The calls were mostly for ice or a bellhop
or to be connected to some number in the outside world.
I'd say, "Just one moment, I'll connect you,"
and move to the next light,
hooking the voices together,
my back to the famous mountains.

In the evenings, music from the lounge
spilled into Reception, and couples would dance their way
into the lobby before heading up to their rooms.
I thought them old and foolish
though I was in love myself.

After work, he and I
would wander around Yosemite Valley.
The chill of the alpine air penetrated our clothes
as we pressed our bodies together
for warmth, for heat—
and swift as the meteors we watched
streaming from Perseus,
we spun out towards the future
where we would quit our jobs
and catch a bus to San Francisco and north to Canada
to what seemed a bigger life
than connecting the voices of strangers
in a place so perfect
it couldn't have been entirely real.

Nineteen

I got married in a black turtleneck
the Summer of Love.
We left our jobs in Yosemite
to live in a hotel in San Francisco,
where the corridors always smelled
like tomato soup, and sometimes
we were hungry enough
it smelled good.

The room clerk
thought we were runaways.
When we said we'd gotten married
just the week before,
some of the residents
offered their congratulations
and shook our hands.

Our room contained a bed
and a fridge: that was about it.
We'd go down the street
to the Chinese bakery
and get almond cookies
(the kind with the whole almond
right on top), eat them
in bed, and wash them down
with orange juice or Guinness.

Frank was older.
He made up
a reading list—
Nietzsche, Pound, Barzun—and gave me
a new name. He'd already had
a nervous breakdown

over another Barbara.
So I became Sibyl.
I was quiet,
and he thought maybe someday
I'd spout out words of wisdom
like the Delphic Oracle.

Of our lovemaking
on that crumb-strewn bed,
my memory is fainter.
And it wasn't too long
before he took
another name himself
and disappeared with a blond woman.

But I remember before
we left Yosemite, standing
at the roadside
waiting to cross
and suddenly I was terrified
—not of what lay ahead with Frank—
but of the joy I was feeling.
I wanted so badly to live
the life ahead of me
that I thought surely
I'd be struck down
before I reached the other side.

And around me,
the lush summer meadows,
the deer lifting their heads without alarm,
before moving to another patch of grass
along the snow-fed river.

The Soldier
for my ex-father-in-law, Frank Justice Bunch Sr.

When all the men were gone,
she led me upstairs
and opened the trunk.
She didn't even look at me
as she lifted out
the few things
buried under blankets and pillowcases.
A ring, a dogtag,
a packet of letters.
He was a soldier who never grew older
than the twenty-some years of his life.
He had never seen his son
and scarcely knew his young wife.

At sixteen she'd run off
to marry him. It was a secret,
but somehow it came out,
and her parents were furious.
There was no honeymoon,
except when they visited his mother.
She gave them the guest bedroom
and in the morning
she brought them breakfast in bed,
poached eggs and toast.

Killed landing on the beaches at Salerno.
One of the letters
was black around the edges,
full of regrets.
His wedding ring
switched for another
less valuable.
One envelope
held all his effects.

I held the hand of his son, my husband,
as we climbed the hill to the cemetery
and weeded the neglected grave,
marked with the headstone of a lamb,
as if he'd died a child.

Professor Miller's Office Hour

Of course you shouldn't drop out,
he said, leaning forward across his desk.
His voice was kind.
Nothing feels relevant anymore,
I told him, but I didn't know what I meant.
Only that since that afternoon
when my husband of a few months
had waved the jagged edge of a broken bottle
in the air, screaming he'd kill the man
who'd splashed us on the dock,
the lines in my literature books
had started to fuzz over
no matter how many times I read them.

I was wearing my favorite skirt,
a hound's-tooth print with tiny black and white squares.
That winter, I wore it almost every day.
Dr. Miller started to quote from Burns:
"John Anderson my jo." *You must know
the poem*, he said. When I shook my head,
he reached the book down from the shelf
and passed it to me. *Here, read it.*
I hadn't said a word about my marriage
but the poem was all about a love
that lasts a lifetime.

Later, after I'd dropped out of school,
I remembered sitting in his office,
the open book across my lap,
my teacher waiting for me to look up.
The pattern in my skirt
blurred behind the words—
and outside, it was raining
like it might never stop.

File Clerk

I stood at the gray bank of files,
sliding *Carlson* in before *Cunningham*,
Lewis after *Lee*, the morning
stretching out endlessly,
low hum of voices in the background:
"I can't believe she'd do that!"
"No, but there's no accounting for
how people . . ." *Wade* before *Wells*.

Just twenty, newly married,
with only the barest of plans.
I wouldn't let myself think: mistake.
His weight on top of me
in the night blotted all that out,
his breath in my ear.

I'd pictured yellow curtains at the windows,
the mantel strewn with wildflowers.
But never this—
the slow days apart, too much time to think,
then the evenings, where the table is laid
and the couple sits down
facing each other
for the long meal.

After

Gaps in the bookshelf.
Empty hangers in the closet.
A sealed letter on the table,
my name written across the front
in his writing.

Then the air in my chest
was no longer enough
as the rest of my life
without him
rushed in to fill the space,
the way matter tries
to even things out,
the way it will not abide
a vacuum.

Divorce

After our polite goodbyes, I go inside
and stand behind the curtain, watching you
as you unlock your bike
and slowly unwind the chain from the banister,
wrapping it around the bike frame
with hands as familiar to me as my own,
hands I knew to measure coffee into the pot,
turn the pages of a book, unbutton my dress.

You are still close enough
to call back,
but I turn away instead to face the room
where once, our life opened to us,
day after day. *Some things
are unbearable,
but we bear them anyway.*
I reach out my hand
for a book, oh let it not be *Tristan and Iseult*
or *Romeo and Juliet*. No,
let it be some tale of clear skies, calm lakes,
mountains that cannot be worn away.

Crossing the Mountains with Blitzen

I have my old horse Blitzen,
but I worry he won't make it
over the mountain pass.
He speaks to me, saying,
Don't worry.

His ribs show through
his dull coat
that once gleamed like dark burnished wood,
and even standing still,
he sways on his feet.

I don't have the courage
to calculate his age
in horse years, so much
swifter than our own.
But because I can't stop what's coming,
I take up the reins:
I lead him
in the direction of the mountains.

Rehearsing Love

I groomed him every day:
black rubber curry comb,
brushes, mane and tail comb,
memorizing those black stockings
down the legs,
the irregular star
on his forehead,
the white triangle on his nose.
He'd watch me, or fall into a doze,
swish his tail,
twitch his skin,
and sigh enormous sighs.

An ex-cutting horse,
used to working for a living,
he must have realized
I was in love
with every inch of him.

I'd scoot under his belly
when I was saddling him,
lie down on his back,
slide off him
over his rump,
like a circus rider.
Sometimes I'd jump on him with no bridle,
let him take me
wherever he wanted to go—
and, at a bone-wrenching trot,
he'd head for his corral
and an early dinner.
On his back, I could enter
any woods, no matter how dark.

And so, when you were born,
my horse-loving daughter,
though I was young,
and had avoided babies,
I knew—to my surprise—what to do.

> *Walk slowly.*
> *Empty yourself*
> *of all cruelty.*
> *What is sent forth as love*
> *returns as love.*
> *Reach out your hand*
> *in good faith.*

Her Legacy
for Aunt Cleone

After the divorce,
she sent me twenty dollars
tucked into the folds
of her crinkly blue stationery
written hard on both sides.
No use crying
over spilt milk, she said,
still, what a shame. There
never had been divorce
in the family. By then,
I had a child
and could barely remember
my aunt's voice, but her certainties
were plain. No leaping
off cliffs for her.
The whir of the sewing machine,
her shelves lined with canned goods
straight from the garden,
that was more her way. Her long letters,
full of other people's news,
never mentioned
my father's silence,
or her own lack of children.
From a quick how are you,
she'd go right to
the surgery of a neighbor
I would never meet,
or what a nice visit
she'd just enjoyed with Elsie.
Who *was* Elsie? I never exactly knew.

But, after all, weren't we all part
of the great messy human family?
It swirled around her kitchen,
where she tied a fresh apron
around her waist,
and carried on.
She would hope for the best,
she concluded before signing her name.
Use the money
for something special.
Something just for you.

At the Begonia Gardens

Working alone, transplanting seedling cacti
from the sandy propagation bed
into one-inch pots, I had to use tweezers
to pick them up, but even so, by the end of an hour,
my hands would be red and throbbing
from touching the spines.

My first day, the foreman handed me a list—
ten pages typed, single spaced—
the Latin names of all the plants in my greenhouse,
and said it would be a good idea if I could learn them,
right away, because those were the names
that would be appearing on the wholesale orders.

Our days were ruled by the break buzzer.
The first blast meant
time to walk to the staff room,
the solitude of the greenhouses shattered,
doors opening on the cold winter air,
people spilling out, all of us walking fast
to the plastic chairs and Coke machine,
time for a quick cup of tea from a thermos,
a little talk among the workers, all women,
hair held back by scarves, rubber boots,
black with red tips.
               "You the new girl?"
"It's hard work, but you get used to it."
Then the warning bell, barely time to walk back
before that last buzzer went off, the one that said,
Be working now or else.

Closing the glass doors behind us,
we'd resume filling the long lists of orders,
packing the pots in square plastic crates,
or watering the long greenhouses,
blowing on our wet hands to keep them warm.

The Cottage

From down here on the beach you can't tell
if it's still there—the row of houses on the cliffs
looks sleek and expensive, nothing like
the shingled cottage with its small garage,
the old De Soto visible through the window,
filling the space, and over the garden gate, a sign
in red wooden letters: Happy Landings.

I remember how I'd leave my own house down the road
and walk that way, often after fights
with the man I lived with
but could never please. I'd stop at the gate:
the old couple was usually outside,
tending the garden that swept towards the cliffs,
sparkle of the bay showing through pine boughs.
Sometimes they were just sitting outside,
chairs pulled close, not talking. And I'd pretend
to tie my shoe or fix my sweater
and just breathe in what was there.

Today I remember the girl I was then,
and realize with a shock I'm nearly old myself,
and yes, I'm happy. I should walk back down that road,
I tell myself, look for the old house, the garden
with its hollyhocks and roses.
The rising tide sends a wave over my bare feet,
and I head back towards my car.
                              But no,
best to leave that desperate girl and that place I loved
as they were. The sun is hot on my back
though it's well into November.

I follow the curve of the beach,
and watch the dogs plunge into the water for sticks or balls,
while sanderlings race back and forth with the waves
as if they were the same ones as always.

On the Water Meridian

He said he treated
the deepest meridian—water—
and tried to explain
the way energy moves through the body,
but I just fell into a sleep
more than sleep,
and, now, driving home along these familiar roads,
I am startled to notice,
as if for the first time,
how the roses lean against the fences,
too heavy to hold themselves up.

All day, their roots have pulled up water,
their leaves made food from sun,
and the petals unleashed their scent
into the bright air.

Passing by in my car,
I feel the pull
toward all this green. My hands
on the steering wheel
look odd to me,
as if, like Daphne, I were changing form,
turning to tree or bush,
and my feet have a restless feeling,
like something was happening far below them:
the summoning of water
to the deep taproots.

The Singer

In that busy café
with the clatter of dishes,
people talking, and bursts of laughter,
there you were,
playing those songs,
some of them centuries old—
"The Wild Colonial Boy,"
"Lakes of Pontchartrain," "Spanish Is a Loving Tongue"—
and, watching you,
I saw that these were the text
you had lived by:
one spark
could light your heart—
and I sipped my coffee
and talked to my friends,
but really, I was listening
to your voice
telling me how things might be,
and though I thought I knew better,
I was listening for my life.

Chinese Food in Calgary

That was the day I decided
to end it: one argument
too many, a sweltering
evening, after two long days
of driving east
through British Columbia,
the logging trucks
roaring past our car,
the smoke of wildfires
stinging our eyes. You shouted
at me in the parking lot,
and, just like that, my heart
snapped shut—
like a purse
with a strong clasp,
never mind what's inside.

But it's an old story:
back in the dorm room
we'd taken to save money,
you apologized,
and we probably made love
on the narrow bunk,
or at least we kissed
and you said
could I ever forgive you,
and was I hungry for dinner
because you were starved.

So we went out,
and it was still light there
even though it was late—
and holding hands,

we looked in the windows
of several places, till we saw
the Chinese place. We sat
next to each other
in a yellow plastic booth,
and over green tea
and jumbo shrimp
served with the traditional yin-yang
of ketchup and hot mustard
on a separate plate,
followed by hot and sour soup
and chicken chow mein,
sprinkled with those crunchy fried noodles
that I love,
everything that was good about us
came back in a flood
no one could have
held back.

And when I broke open
my fortune cookie, it said
"You are lucky
in love." And yours was
something about doors
opening, so we walked out
into the northern night,
and outside it was finally dark,
with the moon
and the swirl of stars.

Villa le Rondini

We walked through those balmy Italian mornings,
past the stone walls,
past the man clearing out the hedgerow
with just a sickle,
past an old woman dressed in black,
her arms full of red roses,
the same roses
that grew everywhere—
and if we walked a little farther,
we could look down on Florence,
the rooftops and the towers,
churchbells, the crazed honking of horns.

Just outside the window,
the young grape vines
twined up the olive trunks,
like arms around a familiar body.
And inside our room,
darkened by the wooden shutters,
the unexpected foreignness
of one another.

Sleeping with You

After a day of too much explaining
how commas work or why it's important
to say exactly what you mean,
followed by errands
and the honking of drivers
needing to get there first, always,
finally, night comes.

Then, in sleep, our bodies curve into one another.
We throw an arm around the other
and sigh or smile, and it's as if
a puzzle of a thousand interlocking pieces—
maybe a Swiss chalet at the foot of the Matterhorn,
a basket of puppies,
or Van Gogh's *Starry Night*—
had been assembled as we slept,
the pieces fitted perfectly into each other,
the picture emerging clear.

Home

Everywhere in Italy
you covered your napkins
with sketches of our dog—
her ears askew,
her tongue lolling out one side,
and that noble profile.

Now, home again,
sitting under the Chinese trees of heaven
and staring up at the varying shades of green
on the hill—greasewood, pine,
avocado, madrone—
I think maybe this
is what love is,
not the suffering for that one word,
that meaningful glance or sudden caress,
but quite simply you,
sitting with one leg
crossed over the other,
your familiar hands
busy at your drawing,
bringing me home
wherever I am.

III.

What the Rain Has Touched

Encounter

When my parents arrive at the door,
they look the same—
my father with his old yellow windbreaker,
my mother's white hair tousled,
but both are a little more stooped, as if
from a tiring journey.
I invite them in, and they sit down together
on the couch, facing me.

I ask them how they are,
but what I really want to ask is,
What's it like to be dead?
I'm afraid that would be rude,
and I'm not sure they even know they're dead,
so we stick to safer topics.
It doesn't matter, though—
all those years of my feeling unseen
and their feeling neglected
have simply dropped away,
and we gaze at each other
in perfect ease.

I turn my head slightly
and, in that instant, they have vanished.
I run to the next room, to tell my husband.
"You won't believe. . ."
and then I can't go on.
I look out the second story window
at the redwoods and the Chinese trees of heaven:
their branches are open to the sky.
Light streams through them.

What I Know About the End of the World

As we drive over Carson Pass and begin
the steep descent down the east side,
the man on the radio is talking
about the end of the world. I look over
the flimsy railing protecting us from the precipice,
just granite above and below us.
If the brakes went out here, I think,
we'd be in that next world,
whatever it may be. I don't have the maps for it,
as he seems to, talking with such zest of the afflictions
soon to befall us before we reach the Rapture.

I think of Frog Lake, not visible from here,
just off the summit of the pass,
exposed to the winds, ringed with stone,
and near enough to the highway
that the sound of the eighteen-wheelers gearing down
as they head over for Carson City or Reno
slices through the quiet.

When I first saw that lake,
I barely stopped for it, but over the years I've noticed
if you time it just right,
you'll come upon the blue iris blooming at the far side.
You'd never expect something that looks so easily broken
could survive at eight thousand feet, where the winds,
even in summer, whip off the snowfields,
or hailstorms rip through on warm afternoons,
and everything that can move
gets out of the way.
But there they are.

Then sometimes the sun
strikes the water in such a way up there
all you want to do
is sit in the shelter of a rock
and watch, leaving everything behind—
the intricacies of this world and the next one, too—
as the wind pushes the ripples of light
in your direction, over and over again.

When
for my dog Molly

I hold her head in my lap,
stroking the muzzle
one last time, running my hands
down the length of her body—
still so perfect, even though the vet says
the cancer is everywhere now.
She looks up at me
and I can't bear the question,
which seems to be simply, *"When?"*

It's a stormy afternoon,
with lashing rains. Her last afternoon
in this world. As the heart-stopping fluid
floods her veins, I bend down to ask her,
what, less than a year later,
I will not be able to ask my own mother:
Wait for me there.
Where you're going. When.

Long Distance from Jerusalem
for my daughter

You've been out on the desert,
you say,
away from phones,
following a dry riverbed
past camps of sleeping Bedouin
in the moonlight.

Last night, here in the Sierras,
the full moon rose over the lake,
making a silver swath;
then a wind sprang up,
scattering the light.
Only the zoom of the bats
diving for mosquitoes
or the occasional plunk of a trout surfacing
broke the quiet.

Knowing you're safe,
something shifts in this landscape,
and as I hang up the phone
and walk back to camp,
I suddenly remember
how at the end of every day,
the light
softens the granite cliffs,
and then the trees
hold onto it
in their highest branches—
as if they could not bear
to let it go
to the other side
of the world.

Mars

Everyone told us
sell him.
He pulled out hitching posts
set in cement;
he bucked my daughter off;
he paced his stall
like a tiger.

Once I dreamed
I was in his stall,
and he became a man.
He was a prisoner.
He wrote poetry
and had a pen-pal.
To me he said,
Lady, I didn't do it.

Now he moves willingly
on the lunge line.
He shifts his gait
according to my daughter's words:
walk, trot, canter,
whoa, reverse.

When she says *come in,*
he walks calmly to her,
waiting to be praised.
Good boy, good boy,
we say, but I wonder
how was the tiger released
from his beautiful body,
the prisoner
from his eyes?

It was so simply accomplished,
here in this green field
near the river.
We reward him with windfall apples
from the tree by the fence.
It is never tended,
but produces year after year
a bountiful crop.

Orion

Orion, caught in the branches
of the Chinese tree of heaven
each November night
as my mother
in the rest home a few miles away
still held to the tangle
of living.

I'd slip outside
not really to draw solace
from the stars
but for the openness,
as if that might
hold some clue:
the cold biting through my nightgown,
distant cries of coyotes,
flap of unseen wings—
probably an owl hunting,
the mouse below fleeing in terror.

But Orion embraced me
each night as he wheeled overhead,
and what I heard
was not the music of the spheres,
but something telling me
how big everything was,
in spite of me.
And so it had been
and would be,
as I stood there,
chilled,

listening to the hugeness of the night,
waiting for my mother
to choose her moment
to go from stardust
back to stardust.

Making Things Right
for my father

Driving through the apple orchards
heavy with fruit,
I realize I have let the anniversary of your death
slip by—ten years already, or is it eleven?
It's a gray morning, and the clouds press down,
obscuring the sun.

I wonder if you knew
when you had to be helped on with your shoes
for the ride to the hospital
that you would never again
stroke your cat
or walk into your lab room
with its walls lined with antique instruments and books.

What I remember most from that time
is standing by your bed
as you grew smaller and smaller,
less and less of you
who had so frightened me as a child,
and looking down at you
lying there quietly
when it was too late to talk.

I just held your hand
and told you I loved you.
I don't know what you heard
or what you knew,
but those words were all that was left
that could matter
before you leapt off
from your bed
in that tiny white room
into something huge.

Mother

A year ago you left messages
on my phone
almost from the other side:
"Come and see this strawberry!
The most beautiful berry
ever. I will save it for you."
And you asked me
to write your checks out,
as if the world of numbers
was suddenly a burden
you would no longer carry—
your signature at the bottom
was enough. It was too hot,
you said. You just couldn't think.
Each breath cost you.

                      But you never
spoke of what was coming
when your tired body
would simply stop.
When you would fly
from earth, all the unsigned checks
abandoned, the strawberry fields
so far below you,
how could they call you back?

The Message

My mother didn't seem to know
quite who I was, the psychic said.
First she thought I was my sister,
and then she said "Becky?"
There had never been anyone
named Becky in our family.
Didn't she remember me,
her own child?
But about some things
she was definite:
"I don't have the hang
of being dead yet," she said.
"I can't believe I'm not alive."

Where was her body,
and the whole physical world—
tables and chairs, dust, crisp apples,
the hard covers of books,
the smell of bread baking?

"But tell her not to worry,"
my mother said. "She
always was the soft-hearted one."
She seemed to have placed me,
though I wondered if "soft-hearted"
was a criticism, if she saw it as
a sign of weakness.

But what about bliss, I asked.
What about being enveloped in light
that was always explained as love,
unconditional love, such as we
could barely imagine?

Well, it doesn't look like bliss,
the psychic said.
But what I see isn't bad,
and—wait—I'm getting something
from your mother again:
"I'm fine.
I'm doing just what
I need to do."

Last night Orion
flung himself sideways across the March sky,
and from deep in the forest,
a great horned owl called,
and was answered, called again,
and what I heard was,
"I love you."
"I'm over here."
Both.

September 12, 2001

The pear tree I planted
in memory of my mother
is suddenly dying:
it tilts,
no longer steady on its roots,
and all its leaves
have gone from green
to almost black. I'm trying
not to read anything particular
into this.

My mother loved pears.
I'd bring her two or three
whenever they were in season.
If they were ripe enough,
we'd cut into one together on the spot
and share the cool, slippery pieces
dripping with sticky juice.

Today there's something sharp and tight
in my chest. I can't tell
if I'm sick or just sad.

How can we ever forget
those images of falling towers?
I keep seeing
the stream of horses
pouring out of Afghanistan,
hip bones jutting out,
their riders urging them on,
trying to get to somewhere safe.

The clouds yesterday hung low and cold
then finally it started to rain.

Lightning cut through the dark sky.
And now, it's warm outside;
the earth smells good.

I say to my mother
(in case she's worried),
It was only a tree. A gopher
must have gnawed at the roots.
I'll plant another tree.
Try again.

A bird crosses the open space
above my head, flying
as birds have always flown.
I rouse the dogs. We'll walk around
and see what the rain has touched.

Looking Up "Ranunculus"

Looking up "ranunculus" in my garden book—
I never can remember
which way to plant them—
I find a note paper-clipped to the page,
in my mother's writing: "China doll,
plant on Olive's shelf"—in her precise script,
only a little shaky.

And though the reference is lost,
I find I cannot throw it away.
It must have been a plant she admired—
and probably wanted—on her neighbor's hall shelf
in the senior apartments.

Without warning,
I am filled with remorse
for all I did not do:
the plants I did not bring her,
the outings we did not take,
time I was unwilling
to give. *I would do it now*, I say,
only it's too late.

I study that note
as if my mother's writing were a code
behind which, a message might spring up:
It's okay, or *I love you, don't worry*—
impossible as the flowers
I know will come forth from these tubers,
breaking open the heavy soil,
yellow, red, purple, unstoppable.

At Lake Margaret, Again
for Mary Lonnberg Smith (1939-1983)

The wind is steady,
rattling the aspen leaves
across the lake,
pushing the water up against the shore.

This time, I don't think
I'll walk around to the other end
to the campsite where I stayed
right after I heard the news.

I can't remember now
how many years have gone by
since that phone call.
But I remember watching
the evening go into night there,
huddled against the mountain cold,
cupping an enamel tin of coffee
in my hands.

Below me, the damselflies
rest on the weeds
as if their brief lives above the water
have already exhausted them.
A water ouzel flies
just above the surface
then lands on a willow branch.

Walking back, I notice
how the aspens along the trail
are slowly healing themselves
from the gashes
of those who have cut their names
into the soft bark—and, off to the side,
a patch of tiger lilies
blazes in the tall grass.

Lake Wilderness

The leaves of the Saggitaria
point in all directions.
I look down and think
yes, they are like arrows
shot with great force.

The leaves are attached to stems
rooted in the silt,
but they float free
as if they were separate—
the way we drift,
my friend and I,
away from the tug of our lives,
and we speak of the past and the future
in barely connected sentences
which we understand perfectly.

The life of the lake continues
as we watch,
as it will continue when we turn away—
water boatmen scurry between the leaves,
tadpoles swim up to the surface,
and the predatory beetle drops from sight.

We lean back against the rock.
Pollen from the lodgepole pines
films the water,
and the delicate damselflies
rise up in pairs, jerkily,
waiting for the next step to be revealed.

Natural History
Seacliff State Beach, Aptos, California

No time for thoughts
or regrets: perhaps a sudden gust of wind
caught the male hawk off guard
as he passed the squirming gopher to his mate,
and then, his wing brushing a power line,
in an instant all three
perished in the air,
falling to the ground
before the eyes of the astonished farmer.

And now, mounted as they were
in that last moment of life,
they hang from the ceiling of the museum.
I study the faces of the birds
for some sign of panic or realization,
but see none, just attention to the task.

Craning my neck to see the display,
I'm suddenly remembering my mother,
her fearful last months
as she approached that edge
closer and closer, clutching tight—
how different from the hawks' free fall
from sky to earth
out of this life.

Cormorants

A hundred feet up,
they sit in the winter sun
their black feathers
sheening gold and brown.

I watch them making their difficult landings
in the thin upper branches of the eucalyptus trees.
The air around the trees
is filled with gravelly calls,
not quite singing or talking,
but something dinosaurs might have heard
in those first days of birds.

The oak trees across the lagoon
are reflected in the still water,
and the late afternoon light
grows softer and softer,
like a thing you could touch.

Nothing lasts is the lesson we have learned
from living on the earth—
yet standing under the cormorant trees,
knowing the sun's light
will give way soon to the light of the stars,
and these birds,
that look like the first birds of the world,
will drift through the night on the high branches,
I feel my life brush
the steadfast life that surrounds my own,
as a bird's wing brushes the air.

Nine Days
for my grandson Israel (May 11, 1998-May 20, 1998)

Bundled against this unseasonably cold spring
that feels more like winter,
my husband and I take long walks,
heading down the steep canyon walls
to the line of green,
the cottonwood and willow
following the curve of the stream.

But no matter how far we walk,
the fact of your not being here
will not soften. Nine days of life
when what we expected
was that you'd be around
long past our own lives.

Everything goes on without you—
the blackbirds, quail,
jackrabbits, and the early wildflowers
blooming along the path—
and even ourselves,
walking through this world
that should have been yours.

With Reptiles
for my grandsons Galil and Hanokh

On a hike up Rattlesnake Mountain,
the boys capture a lizard.
Pet it, Grandma.
See how soft it is?
And look, he likes it.

He does seem to like it.
When I stroke the top of his head,
he closes his eyes for a moment,
then looks around
at the landscape of rocks and artemisia.

I'm remembering
how when I was six or seven
I would slip out to the rose garden
to play with the garter snakes,
tracing the single orange or yellow stripe
that went down the center of their backs.

Light would filter through the feathery acacia leaves,
and the double blossoms of the ornamental cherry
would sway above me
as I spoke to the snakes,
watched for their tongues to answer back,
believing, like the boys,
that we were really talking,
and that they understood.

Evidence

I feel reluctant
to sweep up the redwood needles
I shook from my shoes
after visiting the house
where I grew up.

Maybe they came from
the same trees
I used to run under as a child—
only then my feet
were so tough
I could run barefoot
over the roughest ground
without losing my stride.

But on that November afternoon
I went back, I was wearing shoes,
my coat wrapped tight around me.
Even so, I was cold.

I walked down those roads
I used to know
in every cell of my body,
my sister beside me,
her two tall children ahead of us.
All we could say was
how much smaller everything looked.

Even the redwood—
the one photographed by our father
with us at the base, linking hands
to show its great size—
seemed somehow less.

Now, fingering these brown, sharp needles,
I remember reading how in ancient times
the Chinese nobles saved in sealed jars
every tear they'd ever shed.

Vancouver to Edmonton

Some of the passengers read; others sleep.
Beside me, my husband fills in the squares of his crossword—
word after word taking shape
as fast as he can write. No one
looks out the windows; even the children
are busy doing something else.

But outside, it's like we're in heaven,
with the puffy white clouds,
sun playing along the surface
so bright it's almost impossible to look,
but I look anyway. Then the clouds
give way to a glacial lake,
the aquamarine of a tropical ocean,
then snowfields,
sharp-sided peaks,
and forests so green they are almost black.

The man on the aisle seat
folds up his newspaper. My husband
adds another word
before closing his book.
An announcement comes on
to set our watches ahead an hour.
The toy fields, houses, and barns
take on more reality
as we begin our descent.
There's a green tractor! A barn with a red roof,
cows and horses grazing together. A dog
running out to meet a car.

Whether we were in heaven or not up there
seems beside the point now, as the plane lowers

over fields and highways,
and bumps down on the runway.
Soon we will be rushing out to hail cabs
or scanning the crowds in the airport
for the one familiar face, and the day
will push us forward, with its traffic,
its Mountain Time, its ordinary joys.

Barbara Bloom grew up in California and British Columbia. She earned a bachelor's degree in literature from UC Santa Cruz, a master's degree in English and creative writing from San Francisco State, and has taught composition and creative writing at Cabrillo College for over twenty years. She has a grown daughter and two grandsons and lives with her musician husband and their dog in the countryside south of Santa Cruz. *On the Water Meridian* is her first full-length book.